I0169749

Place

Ulises's

photo here

This book belongs to:

Ulises

# Ulises's Reading Log

## My First 200 Books

**Written and Illustrated by**
**Martha Day Zschock**

**Completed by Ulises**

Commonwealth Editions
Carlisle, Massachusetts

A book is a gift you can
open again and again.

Garrison Keillor

*To Ulises*

Copyright © 2015 Martha Day Zschock
All rights reserved.

978-1-5162-1616-1 paperback
978-1-5162-4116-3 hardcover

Book design by Heather Zschock

Published by Commonwealth Editions
an imprint of Applewood Books
P.O. Box 27, Carlisle, MA 01741

Visit us on the web at www.commonwealtheditions.com
Visit Martha Day Zschock at www.marthazschock.com and
www.growathousandstoriestall.com

Printed in the United States of America

Children are made readers on
the laps of their parents.

Emilie Buchwald

# "Read to Me!"

Reading is important, because if you can read,
you can learn anything about everything and
everything about anything.

Tomie dePaola

The more that you read,
the more things you will know.
The more that you learn,
the more places you'll go.

Dr. Seuss, *Oh, the Places You'll Go!*

# To Ulises's Family...

Experts agree that the best way to prepare children to become readers themselves is to read to them. Learning to read is a process that begins long before your child enters kindergarten. From birth, your baby begins to learn important language and pre-reading skills. As a parent, you are Ulises's first (and favorite) teacher and you are the best person to help your little one learn and grow. When you make reading aloud a daily habit from birth, your child will enter kindergarten ready to read AND ready to succeed. As you record the books that you share, take time to celebrate Ulises's magical journey to becoming a reader!

The years between birth and kindergarten show remarkable growth and transformation. During these early years, your little one is growing and learning constantly. As a parent, you are in a perfect position to provide opportunities for learning through everyday experiences that will foster pre-reading skills.

Each section of this log will explain how reading, playing, singing, talking, and writing can be used to help your child develop important pre-reading skills. You will also find fun and easy tips about how to incorporate these activities into your daily routine in meaningful ways that will help Ulises blossom into a reader! —Martha Zschock

# Ulises's Firsts and Favorites

**Birthday:** _____

**Birthplace:** _____

**How we chose your name:** _____

_____

_____

**On the day you were born:** _____

_____

_____

**Family, Friends, and Special People:** _____

_____

_____

_____

_____

_____

_____

# Sometimes the smallest things take up the most room in your heart.

A.A. Milne, *Winnie the Pooh*

**Favorite Characters:**
_____
_____

**Favorite Songs:**
_____
_____

**Favorite Toys:**
_____
_____

**Favorite Food:**
_____
_____

**First Steps:**
_____
_____

**First Words:**
_____
_____
_____
_____

# Read to me!

Here is where people, one
frequently finds, lower their voices
and raise their minds.

Richard Armour

# Reading Log

1. _____

2. _____

3. _____

4. _____

5. _____

6. _____

7. _____

8. _____

9. _____

10. _____

11. _____

12. _____

13. _____

14. _____

15. _____

Make reading to Ulises
a daily routine. Bedtime? Snack time?
Upon waking up? Choose the
time that works best.

Ask questions as you read. For example,
"What does the cow say?" or, "Can you show me the
blue kite?" Ulises may not be able to answer
today, but soon you'll be in for a surprise!

16. _____

17. _____

18. _____

19. _____

20. _____

21. _____

22. _____

23. _____

24. _____

25. _____

26. _____

27. _____

28. _____

29. _____

30. _____

Once you learn to read,
you will be forever free.

Frederick Douglass

31. _____

32. _____

33. _____

34. _____

35. _____

36. _____

37. _____

38. _____

39. _____

40. _____

41. _____

42. _____

43. _____

44. _____

# Play with Me!

Playing together is not only fun, it's an important time for Ulises to learn and grow. Play offers him the opportunity to learn new skills, experiment with how things work, think creatively, problem solve, develop social skills, practice language, connect to stories, increase comprehension, and learn about the world all around! You are Ulises's favorite playmate, and you can help set the stage for meaningful play that supports his development. Playtime adventures are imaginative and magical. When learning is fun, your child learns best!

Creative play is like a spring that bubbles up from deep within a child.

Joan Almon, *Alliance for Childhood*

45. _____

46. _____

47. _____

48. _____

49. _____

50. _____

51. _____

52. _____

53. _____

54. _____

55. _____

56. _____

57. _____

58. _____

59. _____

60. _____

Play "rhyme time" during the day. Say a word and help
Ulises think of others that rhyme with it.
You can use prompts such as,
"I saw a cat sit on a _____."

Go on a color walk. Choose a color and let
Ulises find things that match.

61. _____

62. _____

63. _____

64. _____

65. _____

66. _____

67. _____

68. _____

69. _____

70. _____

71. _____

72. _____

73. _____

# Sing to Me!

Singing and clapping to the beat are fun ways to add learning to your daily routine! Children naturally respond to music. Babies are soothed by the gentle sounds of a lullaby, and boisterous toddlers love to jump to the beat. Singing slows down language, making it easier to hear distinct sounds in words. Rhythms allow children to hear syllables in words. Jazzy tunes encourage dancing and clapping, which strengthens motor skills. Songs can also introduce new ideas and concepts. They often have repetitive words, rhymes, and verses which reinforce learning. Rhymes, letters, numbers, days of the week, animal sounds, and shapes—many things can be taught through songs.

*If you're happy and you know it,
clap your hands!*

74. _____

75. _____

76. _____

77. _____

78. _____

79. _____

80. _____

81. _____

82. _____

83. _____

84. _____

85. _____

86. _____

87. _____

Sing throughout the day—when Ulises
wakes up or as you go for a walk or ride in the car.
Make music part of Ulises's daily life.

...you do not leave a library; if you do what it wants you to do, you are taking it with you.

Elie Wiesel

88. _____

89. _____

90. _____

91. _____

92. _____

93. _____

94. _____

# Talk to Me!

It might feel strange to talk to a baby who can't yet speak, but don't let that stop you! Talking with your child throughout the day is very important. Babies learn to talk by hearing those around them speak. As children listen, they learn sounds, words, expressions, and gestures that make up language. Talking with children extends their vocabulary, and increases their understanding of the world. Reading and language development go hand in hand. When you have conversations with Ulises, ask questions, explain how things work, name things, tell stories, point out letters and numbers, and describe things; you are helping him make connections between spoken and written language.

The sound of a word is at least as important as the meaning.

Jack Prelutsky

95. _____

96. _____

97. _____

98. _____

99. _____

100. _____

101. _____

102. _____

103. _____

104. _____

105. _____

106. _____

107. _____

108. _____

109. _____

110. _____

Speak to Ulises in your native language. Children learn best when language is spoken fluently.

# A B C D

111. _____

112. _____

113. _____

114. _____

115. _____

116. _____

117. _____

118. _____

119. _____

120. _____

121. _____

122. _____

123. _____

124. _____

125. _____

RED SQUARE

BLUE
ORANGE
GREEN

RED
PURPLE
YELLOW

# Write with Me!

Writing, reading, speaking, and listening are all forms of communication. To be able to write, children need to understand that written words are symbols of spoken words, and that writing has a purpose. They also need to develop fine motor skills and hand-eye coordination necessary to form letters, words, and pictures. There are many small ways throughout the day that you can help your child become a writer! Help Ulises notice words, letters, numbers, shapes, and colors in books and in the world all around. Let him see you write and explain what you are doing. Provide opportunities to play with small objects, such as blocks, puzzles, and beads to strengthen small muscles in his fingers and hands. From the very first scribbles Ulises is attempting to communicate, and you can help foster this magical progression from early lines to written words!

What wonderful paints and brushes
they had! George could not resist.

H.A. Rey, *Curious George*

# W X Y Z

126. _____

127. _____

128. _____

129. _____

130. _____

131. _____

132. _____

133. _____

134. _____

135. _____

136. _____

137. _____

138. _____

139. _____

140. _____

Children love to see their names in print.
Say each letter as you write Ulises's name.
Label your child's belongings and artwork!

Make a special box for writing supplies.
Fill it with crayons, markers, child-friendly scissors,
paper, stickers, paints, and glue sticks.

141. _____

142. _____

143. _____

144. _____

145. _____

146. _____

147. _____

148. _____

149. _____

150. _____

151. _____

152. _____

153. _____

154. _____

155. _____

156. _____

157. _____

158. _____

159. _____

160. _____

161. _____

162. _____

163. _____

164. _____

165. _____

166. _____

167. _____

168. _____

169. _____

170. _____

There is no frigate
like a book
To take
us lands away...

Emily Dickinson

Staple sheets of paper together to make a book!
Ulises can write and illustrate
his own story!

171. _____

172. _____

173. _____

174. _____

175. _____

176. _____

177. _____

178. _____

179. _____

180. _____

181. _____

182. _____

183. _____

184. _____

185. _____

186. _____

187. _____

188. _____

189. _____

190. _____

191. _____

192. _____

193. _____

194. _____

195. _____

196. _____

197. _____

198 _____

199. _____

200. _____

Be a role model!
Let Ulises
see you reading too!

Yay
Ulises!
**200**
BOOKS!

# Congratulations!

Hooray for Ulises! You did it!
You read 200 books!

Place photo here

Anything can happen, child.
Anything can be.

Shel Silverstein, *Where the Sidewalk Ends*

# Ulises's Top 10 Favorite Books

1. _____

_____

2. _____

_____

3. _____

_____

4. _____

_____

5. _____

_____

**6.** _____

_____

**7.** _____

_____

**8.** _____

_____

**9.** _____

_____

**10.** _____

_____

The journey of a thousand miles
begins with one step.

Lao Tzu

# Special family and friends who read with me!

For further resources, tips, and ideas visit our website at

www.growathousandstoriestall.com

## Other Read to Me! Books and Materials from Martha Day Zschock

# My First Reading Log

Watch your child grow a thousand stories tall! This hardover edition has room for 1,000 books and includes goodies galore to motivate the little reader.

*My First Reading Log includes:*

- Reward stickers to celebrate reading milestones
- A four-foot growth chart to measure reading progress
- More fun and colorful illustrations, tips, and inspiring quotes
- More places for photos, first words, favorite foods, and special dates

ISBN 978-1-938700-29-3 • $14.95
Hardcover • 6 x 9 • 104 pp

# My Reading Growth Chart

Unfold this four-foot growth chart to measure your child's reading progress and physical growth. Included with the hardcover edition of *My First Reading Log* and sold separately.

ISBN 978-1-938700-31-6 • $3.95
1 7/8 x 54 • 2 pp

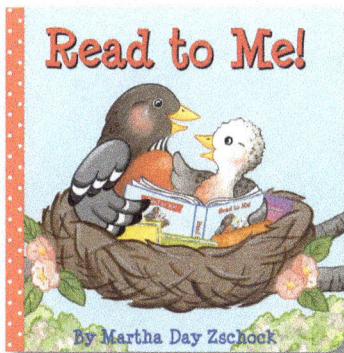

# Read to Me!

Created to encourage a love of reading in the very youngest children, *Read To Me!* is, with its rhymes and colorful illustrations, a wonderful book to read aloud, for the reader and the listener. The shared experience is sure to create an appreciation of books, and encourages children and their family and friends to read together. For ages 2-5.

ISBN 978-1-938700-27-9 • $7.95
Board book • 6 x 6 • 16 pp

To Order: 800-277-5312 or visit awb.com

www.ingramcontent.com/pod-product-compliance
Lightning Source LLC
Chambersburg PA
CBHW071652050426
42443CB00026B/3174